Question Time

Reptiles

Claire Llewellyn

KING*f*ISHER

NEW YORK

Editor: Jennie Morris
Coordinating Editors: Denise Heal, Sarah Snavely
Designer: John Jamieson
DTP Coordinator: Sarah Pfitzner
Consultants: Claire Robinson, Norah Granger
Indexer: Jason Hook
Production Controller: Debbie Otter
Illustrators: Chris Forsey 10–11, 12–13, 24–25;
Craig Greenwood 17cr, 17tr; **Ray Grinaway** 8–9, 22–23;
Ian Jackson 11tr; **David Marshall** 21tr; **Nicki Palin** 14–15c;
Bernard Robinson 16–17bl; **Mike Rowe** 6–7, 18–19, 26–27;
Roger Stewart 28–29; **David Wright** 4–5, 20bl, 21cl.
Cartoons: Ian Dicks
Picture Research Manager: Jane Lambert
Picture Research Assistant: Rachael Swann
Picture Acknowledgments: 5cr Jean-Louis Le Moigne/NHPA;
7tr Francois Gohier/Ardea London; **9**cr Z. Leszczynski/www.osf.uk.com;
13tr J.A.L. Cooke/www.osf.uk.com; **15**tr Daniel Heuclin/NHPA;
19cr Martin Withers/Frank Lane Picture Agency; **22**tr Francois
Gohier/Ardea London; **27**cr Mark Jones/www.osf.uk.com;
29tr Nigel J. Dennis/NHPA.
Artwork Archivists: Wendy Allison, Steve Robinson

*Every effort has been made to trace the copyright holders of the photographs.
The publishers apologize for any inconvenience caused.*

KINGFISHER
a Houghton Mifflin Company imprint
215 Park Avenue South
New York, New York 10003
www.houghtonmifflinbooks.com

First published in 2002
10 9 8 7 6 5 4 3 2 1

1TR/0502/TIMS/RNB(RNB)/128MA

LIBRARY OF CONGRESS CATALOGING-IN-PUBLICATION DATA
has been applied for.

ISBN 0-7534-5451-3 (HC)
ISBN 0-7534-5463-7 (PB)

Printed in China

CONTENTS

ABOUT this book

Have you ever wondered what the difference between alligators and crocodiles is? Have all your questions answered, and learn other fascinating facts on every information-packed page of this book. Words in **bold** are in the glossary on page 31.

Look and find
★ ★
eye

All through the book, you will see the **Look and find** symbol. This has the name and picture of a small object that is hidden somewhere on the page. Look carefully to see if you can find it.

Now I know . . .

★ This box contains quick answers to all of the questions.

★ They will help you remember all about the amazing world of reptiles.

Look and find head

WHAT
is a reptile?

Snakes, lizards, tortoises, and crocodiles belong to a group of animals called reptiles. Reptiles are all **cold-blooded**, and they all have skeletons and tough skins made of plates or scales. Most reptiles lay eggs. Their eggs are always laid on dry land and have hard or leathery shells.

Snake

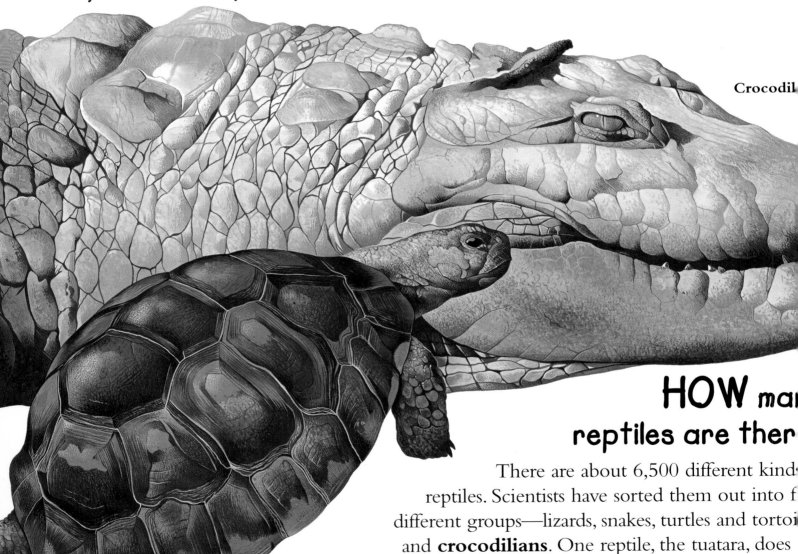

Crocodil

Tortoise

HOW mar
reptiles are ther

There are about 6,500 different kind reptiles. Scientists have sorted them out into f different groups—lizards, snakes, turtles and tortoi and **crocodilians**. One reptile, the tuatara, does fit into any of these groups. It is a rare, lizard creature that is found only in New Zeala

4

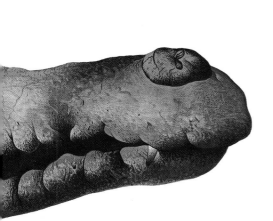

WHICH reptiles are record breakers?

Two record-breaking reptiles are the saltwater crocodile and the anaconda snake. A large saltwater crocodile is longer and heavier than two cars parked end to end. An anaconda can grow up to 33 ft. (10m) long and can be as heavy as a cow. But some reptiles are tiny—one lizard in the West Indies is no bigger than your thumb!

Lizard

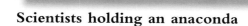

Scientists holding an anaconda

hat's amazing!

...re are only 22 kinds of crocodilians ...about 3,800 kinds of lizards!

...e reptiles live for a very long ...Giant tortoises ...live for 120 ...rs or more!

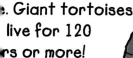

WHERE do reptiles live?

Reptiles live in many different **habitats**, including deserts, **rain forests**, swamps, rivers, and even in the ocean. Some reptiles live in dark, damp caves or in underground burrows. Reptiles are found in most parts of the world except for very cold places. But the greatest number live in the **tropics**, where the climate is warm all year round.

WHY do crocodiles bask in the sun?

Crocodiles feel sluggish after the cool night, so they bask in the morning sun. As their body temperature starts to rise they become more active. Later, when the crocodiles get too hot, they cool off in the river or in the shade. Like all reptiles they are cold-blooded—they control their body temperature by moving between warmer and cooler places.

Nile crocodiles basking on a riverbank

WHICH snakes sleep all winter long?

Garter snakes live in places where the winters are cold. In the fall, as the days grow cooler, the snakes begin to feel drowsy and look for a safe, dry hole in the ground. When they find one, they curl up and sleep until the spring. This long rest is known as **hibernation**. Many different kinds of snakes hibernate—some for up to eight months a year!

Red-sided garter snakes leaving their hibernation den

That's amazing!

Crocodiles cool down by opening their mouths and letting the breeze blow inside!

Up to 1,000 rattlesnakes may hibernate together—usually in the same place every year!

Crocodiles allow small birds called plovers to go inside their mouths to feed on **parasites** and leftover scraps of food.

Now I know . . .

★ Reptiles live in many different habitats all over the world.
★ Crocodiles bask in the sun to raise their temperature.
★ Snakes in cold places usually sleep all winter long.

WHICH is
the largest lizard?

Komodo dragons are enormous lizards that live on some of the islands in Southeast Asia. From snout to tail they measure about 1.9 ft. (3m) long. These lizards are **scavengers**, but they also kill pigs, goats, and deer by infecting them with deadly **saliva**. Any animal bitten by a Komodo dragon will die.

That's amazing!

Some lizards that lose their tail go ba later to find it—and eat it!

Some lizards run on their two back le The basilisk lizard of South America can even run across water!

Komodo dragons have long claws and short, powerful legs. They can swim, climb trees, and run as fast as an athlete—up to 11 mph (18km/h).

Komodo dragons

Geckos have no eyelids to keep their eyes clean—they use their tongues to wipe away sand and dirt.

HOW do geckos walk on the ceiling?

Geckos are small, tropical lizards that often live in people's houses. You can see them running up walls and windows and across the ceiling. They can walk upside down without falling off because of ridged pads on the bottom of their feet. These pads are made up of tiny hooked hairs that help give the geckos a great grip on surfaces.

WHY do some lizards lose their tails?

Predators catch some lizards by their tails. The tail is sometimes the only part of a lizard's body that predators can grab. When this happens, a lizard can still escape by breaking off the end of its tail. This trick surprises the predator and gives the lizard time to run away. This lizard's tail (below) looks a little stumpy, but it will soon start to regrow.

Southeastern five-lined skink losing its tail

Now I know . . .

★ The largest lizard is the Komodo dragon.
★ Geckos can walk on the ceiling because of pads on the bottom of their feet.
★ Some lizards lose their tails to escape from predators.

9

★ Look and find ★
teeth

HOW do crocodiles catch a meal?

Crocodiles catch a meal by sneaking up on it. They hide underwater, sealing their eyes, ears, nostrils, and throat with special waterproof flaps. When an animal comes to the water to drink, it cannot see or smell the crocodile. Suddenly the crocodile explodes out of the water, grabs the animal, and drowns it.

WHERE would you find a saltie?

"Saltie" is the nickname that Australians give to the saltwater crocodile. Most crocodilians live in freshwater, but salties are found in **estuaries**, swamps along the coast, and even far out at sea. A saltie's body is covered with thinner, lighter scales than other crocodilians, and these help it swim more easily.

Saltwater crocodile attacking

Crocodiles can only swallow—not chew—their food. They shake their **prey** from side to side in their powerful jaws until it breaks into bite-size pieces.

WHAT is the difference between alligators and crocodiles?

Some crocodilians are hard to tell apart. An alligator's snout is broad and rounded, while a crocodile's is thinner and more pointed. Unlike on an alligator, a large tooth sticks out from a crocodile's jaw when its mouth is shut. Some crocodilians are easier to recognize—gavials have a very slender snout, which is perfect for grabbing fish.

Alligator

Crocodile

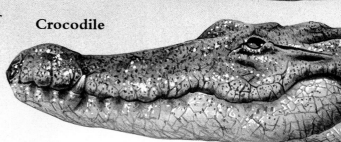

Gavial

That's amazing!

Crocodilians are always growing new teeth. If any teeth are lost during an attack, new ones grow in their place!

Male alligators bellow loudly in the breeding season to keep their rivals away!

Wallaby

Now I know . . .

★ Crocodiles hide underwater to catch a meal.

★ Australian "salties" are found in estuaries, swamps, and the sea.

★ Alligators and crocodiles have different-shaped snouts.

WHAT is the difference between tortoises and turtles?

Tortoises and turtles look very similar, but there are some differences. Tortoises have stumpy feet and live on land. Turtles have flippers, flatter shells, and live in the ocean. Both tortoises and turtles have hard, horny beaks. Tortoises eat juicy plants, while turtles snap up sea creatures. Turtles that live in rivers and streams are called terrapins.

Loggerhead turtle

Mother and baby starred tortoise

HOW fast can a tortoise crawl?

A tortoise's shell is like a suit of armor and is a heavy load to wear. Because of this tortoises crawl along slowly at about 0.3 mph (0.5km/h). Because turtles are lifted up by the salty water of the sea, they do not have to carry their own weight. They can swim over 19 mph (30km/h)— as fast as you could ride your bicycle!

12

WHICH terrapin is a crafty fisherman?

When an alligator snapping turtle feels hungry, it lies on the riverbed and opens its beak. On its tongue is a wriggly flap of skin that looks just like a worm. Hungry fish swim up to the "worm" and are snapped up by the terrapin's sharp beak. These terrapins are named after alligators because they were once thought to be a cross between a terrapin and an alligator.

Alligator snapping turtle fishing

Every kind of tortoise has its own special shell pattern. This makes it stand out from other **species**. It also helps **camouflage** the animal, making it harder for predators such as birds and foxes to see it.

That's amazing!

Tortoises have lived on earth for at least 200 million years!

Some terrapins have an air tube on the end of their nose that sticks out like a snorkel!

Now I know . . .

★ Tortoises have feet and live on land. Turtles have flippers and live in the ocean.
★ Tortoises go 0.3 mph (0.5km/h).
★ The alligator snapping turtle has a smart way of catching fish.

WHICH snakes shed their skins?

They all do! A snake's skin does not grow with the rest of its body, so as the animal gets bigger its skin becomes too tight. Every few months it sheds its top layer of scales. Underneath it has a brand-new skin in a better-fitting size.

A snake's skin splits at the snout and peels off like a long, scaly sock. A snake begins to shed its skin by rubbing its snout against a rough surface such as a branch or a stone.

HOW do snakes find their prey?

Snakes use their senses to track down their prey. They have good eyesight, and their flickering, forked tongues pick up smells in the air. Some snakes have an extra sense—tiny holes on the sides of their faces pick up the warmth of animals close by.

Snakes' eyes never close because they have no eyelids. Their eyes are protected by a see-through scale.

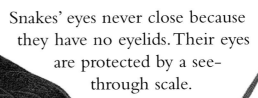

14

Emerald tree boa shedding its skin

Brown tree snake showing its fangs

WHY do snakes have fangs?

Some snakes, such as boomslangs and cobras, have a pair of sharp, hollow **fangs**. Snakes use their fangs to inject poison into their prey. The poison is made in **glands** inside their cheeks. When a snake attacks, the **venom** is squeezed along a narrow tube and out through the deadly fangs.

That's amazing!

No snakes are plant-eaters—they all need meat to survive!

We have 29 bones in our backbone— a snake can have up to 400!

Now I know . . .

★ All snakes shed their skins several times a year.
★ Snakes have sharp senses to help them find their prey.
★ Some snakes kill by injecting poison through their fangs.

15

WHERE do turtles lay their eggs?

Female turtles lay their eggs in holes on sandy beaches. Two months later the eggs hatch, and the tiny turtles dig up to the surface and scuttle to the sea. They have to hurry or they will be eaten by seagulls and other predators.

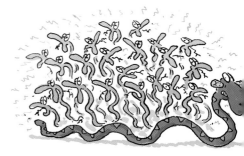

That's amazing!

Rattlesnakes have about 10 babies at a time, but other snakes can have up to 40!

Turtles lay their eggs on moonlit nights. Each turtle lays about 100 eggs before returning to the sea.

WHAT is a snakeling?

A snakeling is a baby snake. Most snakes lay eggs but others, such as boa constrictors and some vipers, are **viviparous** and give birth to live young. As with most other reptiles the mother does not take care of her young. Some snakelings have sharp fangs and venom, and they can take care of themselves!

Snakeling hatching

WHY are crocodiles such good mothers?

Female crocodiles guard their nests. When they hear their babies calling, the mothers open the nest and help their young hatch, and then they gently carry them to the riverbank in their jaws.

Crocodile carrying babies tenderly in her mouth

Now I know . . .

★ Turtles lay their eggs in holes on sandy beaches.
★ A snakeling is a baby snake.
★ Crocodiles, unlike most reptiles, care for their young after they hatch.

WHERE does the leaf-tailed gecko hide?

The leaf-tailed gecko hides on tree branches. It has a ragged shape, flat body, barklike skin, and a tail shaped like a leaf. These features help it blend in with its background. Camouflage helps animals like the gecko hide from predators. But camouflage can help hunters too by hiding them from their prey!

These leaf-tailed geckos live in the rain forests of Australia and Madagascar, an island the east coast of Afri

WHY are coral snakes so brightly colored?

All animals can clearly see the coral snake with its bright red, black, and white stripes. The bold colors warn other animals that the snake is venomous and will hurt them if they attack it. The warning keeps predators away and helps coral snakes avoid danger.

Colorful coral snake

HOW do chameleons stay out of sight?

Chameleons have an amazing way of hiding—their skin color changes to match their surroundings. When this lizard moves, **cells** in its skin change size, moving grains of color closer to the surface or deeper beneath it. It takes about five minutes for a chameleon to change its color completely.

Green skin is the perfect camouflage for a flap-necked chameleon in the trees.

at's amazing!

milk snake has the same color stripes the deadly coral snake—just in a different ler. Although it is harmless, other nals think it is venomous keep out of way!

A chameleon's tongue is as long as its body! And it has a sticky tip to grab flies and other insects!

Now I know . . .

★ Leaf-tailed geckos hide on tree branches.
★ Coral snakes are brightly colored to warn other animals that they are dangerous.
★ Chameleons stay out of sight by changing their skin color.

19

Look and find rattle

HOW does the frilled lizard trick its enemies?

When a frilled lizard is threatened by predators, it raises a flap of skin around its neck, opens its mouth, and hisses. But this is just a useful trick. The lizard is actually harmless, but it makes itself look big and fierce to frighten away its enemies!

By raising its flap of skin a frilled lizard looks about four times larger than it really is.

WHY does a rattlesnake rattle?

large animals get too close to a rattlesnake, it tries to warn them away. It makes a buzzing sound shaking the dry, scaly rings the tip of its tail. As soon as imals hear this sound they ove out of harm's way.

Rattlesnake shaking its rattle

Chuckwalla jammed between two rocks

WHICH lizard gets itself into a jam?

The chuckwalla lives in rocky deserts in the United States. When it is frightened, it hides in a crack in a rock. Then it sucks in air and puffs up its body, jamming itself in so tightly that it cannot be pulled out.

That's amazing!

The Australian blue-tongued skink scares its enemies by sticking out its extraordinary blue tongue!

The grass snake is a great actor. It fools its enemies by pretending to be dead!

Now I know ...

★ The frilled lizard tricks its enemies by making itself look fierce.
★ Rattlesnakes rattle their tails to warn away other animals.
★ The chuckwalla squeezes itself between cracks in rocks.

HOW does a caiman catch fish?

Caimans live in the marshes and streams of South American rain forests. They feed on slippery prey, such as frogs and fish. Their teeth are sharp, and they curve back toward their throat. This helps them grab the fish that dart along the fast-flowing streams.

A spectacled caiman snaps up a f
Caimans also feed on shrimp, sna
birds, and small **mammals**.

**A gaboon viper
waiting for prey**

WHERE do gaboon vipers hide?

Gaboon vipers hide out of sight on the rain forest floor. The pattern of their skin works well to camouflage them against the brown dead leaves. The vipers lie still, watching and waiting, until a bird or other animal comes along. Then they strike—wounding their prey with their long sharp fangs and injecting it with poison.

22

aboon viper's fangs are up
2 in. (5cm) long—about the size
of your thumb!

en a
adise
e snake
nts to "fly," it spreads
t its back, sucks in its
mach, and glides
ough the air!

A flying lizard
leaps with the help
of its "wings."

WHICH
lizard has wings?

The flying lizard lives in the
rain forests of Southeast Asia.
On the sides of its body are flaps of
skin that fan out when it leaps from
a tree. These "wings" help the lizard
escape from predators and pounce
on flies and other insect prey.

Now I know . . .

★ A caiman catches fish
with its pointed teeth.
★ Gaboon vipers hide on
the rain forest floor.
★ The flying lizard has
flaps of skin called "wings"
that help it glide.

23

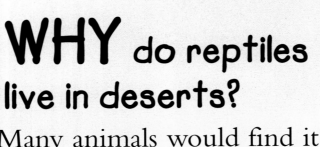

Look and find
★ ★
desert rabbit

WHY do reptiles live in deserts?

Many animals would find it hard to live in a desert, but reptiles are well-equipped to life in this harsh, dry habitat. Their thick, scaly skin locks in every drop of water and stops them from drying out. And because their energy comes from the sun, they can survive on very little food.

WHAT is the best way of moving over sand?

It can be tricky moving over loose, sandy ground—it is easy to sink into the sand instead of moving forward! The sidewinder rattlesnake has solved this problem by using a movement known as sidewinding. It forms its body into S-shaped loops and moves itself sideways over the ground.

Sidewinder rattlesnake

Desert iguana

Regal horned lizard

Kangaroo rat

OW does a desert tortoise
ol down?

e desert tortoise avoids the hottest part of
e day by hiding in an underground burrow.
t does get caught in the sun, the tortoise
inates on its back two legs. As the urine dries
in the desert air, it cools the animal down.

That's amazing!

The thorny devil from
Australia is never
thirsty—it drinks
the dew that runs
off its spines!

A desert tortoise can go more than
a year without a sip of water!

Desert tortoises

Gila monster

Now I know ...

★ Reptile bodies are well-adapted to desert life.
★ Moving sideways is a good way of moving over sand.
★ The desert tortoise cools down by urinating on itself.

Look and find foot

WHICH lizard eats underwater?

The marine iguana is the only lizard that eats underwater. It lives on the Galapagos Islands near Ecuador. It dives into the sea to eat the seaweed that grows on rocks below the surface of the water. Marine iguanas can stay underwater for about one hour.

WHY do sea snakes have flat tails?

The sea snake's flat tail helps it swim. It works like a paddle and moves the animal quickly through the water. Some sea snakes swim out in the open ocean. Others, such as kraits, stay near the coast. They dive to the seabed and search for fish among the rocks.

Blue-footed boobies

Marine iguanas

Yellow-bellied sea snake

Sally Lightfoot crab

hat's amazing!

rine iguanas stay warm
night by piling on top
one another!

snakes are the
rld's most venomous
kes—they kill more
ple than any other
creature!

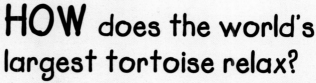

HOW does the world's largest tortoise relax?

The world's largest tortoise, the giant tortoise, lives on the Galapagos Islands. These **volcanic** islands have large pools that are heated by underground rocks. The tortoises like to relax in the warm water just like we do when we take a bath!

Giant tortoises wallow in the warm, volcanic pools

Now I know . . .

★ The marine iguana is the only lizard that eats underwater.

★ Sea snakes have flattened tails that help them swim.

★ Giant tortoises relax in warm, volcanic pools.

WHY are turtles in danger?

Turtles are in danger of becoming **extinct**. Thousands are hunted by people for their meat and shells, while others drown accidentally when they are caught in fishing nets. Turtles are also producing fewer young than before. This is because the females are disturbed by the noise and lights of hotels near their nesting grounds. Scientists help turtles by removing their eggs from busy beaches. They take them to a safe place to hatch.

These baby turtles hatched from eggs that were collected and taken care of by scientists. Now the turtles can enter the sea safe from birds and other predators.

hat's amazing!

Chinese alligator is in danger of extinction—
a few hundred survive in the wild!

giant tortoise needs protection—its eggs
young are eaten by pigs and dogs that
ple brought to the Galapagos Islands!

OW can we help reptiles?

e best way to help reptiles is to study
m, understand how they live, and teach
er people about them. Special laws can
p protect reptiles and the habitats where
y live. Zoos can also help reptiles by
eding back-up populations that
be released into the wild.

een turtle
tchlings

Feeding time at a crocodile sanctuary

WHO hunts crocodilians?

Crocodilians are hunted by people
who sell their skins. The skins are used
to make products such as purses, belts, and
shoes. Some countries have lost so many
crocodilians that they are now protected by
law. The rarest species are kept in crocodile
sanctuaries so that they can breed in peace.

Now I know . . .

★ Turtles are in danger because
of hunting, fishing, and tourism.
★ We can help reptiles by
studying them, protecting their
habitats, and helping them breed.
★ People hunt crocodilians.

29

REPTILES QUIZ

What have you remembered about reptiles? Test what you know, and see how much you have learned.

1 What type of reptile is a gavial?
a)   a lizard
b)   a crocodilian
c)   a snake

2 Which reptile changes the color of its skin?
a)   a leaf-tailed gecko
b)   a coral snake
c)   a chameleon

3 In what habitat do gaboon vipers live?
a)   in the rain forest
b)   in the desert
c)   in the sea

4 Which reptiles shed their skin?
a)   crocodilians
b)   tortoises
c)   snakes

5 Where do giant tortoises live?
a)   the Galapagos Islands
b)   Madagascar
c)   the desert

6 Which reptile kills with its deadly saliva?
a)   chuckwalla
b)   Komodo dragon
c)   garter snake

7 Where do salties live?
a)   in the desert
b)   in rivers and the sea
c)   in the rain forest

8 Which reptile has a tail like a paddle?
a)   sea snake
b)   marine iguana
c)   turtle

9 How long do turtle eggs take to hatch?
a)   two days
b)   two weeks
c)   two months

10 What part of a rattlesnake rattles?
a)   its tail
b)   its fangs
c)   its tongue

Find the answers on page 32.

GLOSSARY

eding Having young.

nouflage The color, shape, pattern of an animal's body, ch help it blend in with its roundings. A camouflaged nal is very hard to see.

s The tiny living units make up an animal's body.

d-blooded Having a body perature that changes with surrounding temperature.

codilians A group of iles that includes crocodiles, ators, caimans, and gavials.

aries Places where the water of a river meets saltwater of the sea.

nct When a type of animal longer living on earth.

fangs Long, sharp, hollow teeth that some snakes use to inject venom into their prey.

glands Parts of the body that make a special substance, such as venom.

habitats The natural homes of animals or plants.

hibernation The long, deep sleep that helps many animals survive the winter in cold parts of the world.

mammals Warm animals with bony skeletons that feed their young milk. Dogs, bats, and whales are all mammals.

parasites Animals or plants that live on another animal or plant.

predators Animals that hunt other animals for food.

prey Animals that are hunted and killed by other animals.

rain forests Thick, tropical forests with very heavy rainfall.

saliva The watery juice inside an animal's mouth.

scavengers Animals that eat dead or dying animals.

species Particular types of animals or plants.

tropics The warmest parts of the world. They are near the equator.

urinates Passes waste liquid called urine out of the body.

venom The poison that some snakes and other animals inject into their prey.

viviparous Giving birth to live young. The young develop inside the mother's body and do not hatch from an egg.

volcanic Made by volcanoes.

INDEX

Answers to the Reptiles Quiz

★ 1 b ★ 2 c ★ 3 a ★ 4 c ★ 5 a ★ 6 b ★ 7 b ★ 8 a ★ 9 c ★ 10 a